GLOBAL WARMING AND THE DINOSAURS

FOSSIL DISCOVERIES AT THE POLES

by CAROLINE ARNOLD • Illustrated by LAURIE CAPLE

Clarion Books

Houghton Mifflin Harcourt

Boston • New York

2009

For Alessandra, Lucas, and Paige —C.A.

For Catherine, Lynda, Melissa, and our Shattuck village —L.C.

I would like to thank Dr. Patricia Vickers Rich of the Monash Science Centre, Monash University, Clayton, Victoria, Australia, and Dr. Tom Rich, senior curator of Vertebrate Palaeontology, Museum Victoria, Melbourne, Australia, for reading and critiquing the manuscript. I also thank Dr. Anthony Fiorillo at the Museum of Nature and Science in Dallas, Texas, for his assistance. Many scientists, including Dr. Roland Gangloff, principal investigator and curator of research at the University of Alaska Museum, Fairbanks, Alaska, and Dr. William R. Hammer, Department of Geology at Augustana College, Rock Island, Illinois, have done pioneering work in the relatively new area of polar paleontology. I am grateful for their research reports as sources of information for this book.

The illustrator would also like to thank Dr. William R. Hammer, Department of Geology, Augustana College; Susan Kornreich Wolf, associate curator and educational programs coordinator, Fryxell Geology Museum, Augustana College; and Margaret Triffitt, Western Australian Museum, Welshpool DC, Australia, for their expert advice.

Clarion Books
215 Park Avenue South, New York, New York 10003
Text copyright © 2009 by Caroline Arnold
Illustrations copyright © 2009 by Laurie Caple

The illustrations were executed in watercolor.
The text was set in 13-point Giovanni Book.

Clarion Books is an imprint of Houghton Mifflin Harcourt Publishing Company.

www.clarionbooks.com

Printed in Singapore

Library of Congress Cataloging-in-Publication Data
Arnold, Caroline.
Global warming and the dinosaurs : fossil discoveries at the poles / by Caroline Arnold ; illustrated by Laurie Caple.
p. cm.
Includes index.
ISBN: 978-0-618-80338-5
[1. Dinosaurs—North Pole—Juvenile literature. 2. Dinosaurs—South Pole—Juvenile literature.
3. Paleoclimatology—North Pole—Juvenile literature. 4. Paleoclimatology—South Pole—Juvenile literature.
5. Paleontology—Mesozoic—Juvenile literature.] I. Caple, Laurie A., ill. II. Title.
QE861.5.A776 2009
567.90911—dc22
2008026651

TWP 10 9 8 7 6 5 4 3 2 1

Dinosaur on cover: *Cryolophosaurus ellioti*; dinosaur on this page: *Pachyrhinosaurus*;
title page: Mount Kirkpatrick, Antarctica.

Contents

DINOSAURS AT EARTH'S EXTREMES — 4

A WARMER WORLD — 6

  Surviving Winter — 8

    Staying Warm — 8

    Seeing in the Dark — 9

DISCOVERING FOSSILS — 10

DINOSAURS OF THE FAR NORTH — 12

  Alaska — 12

    A Herd of Hadrosaurs — 14

    Crests, Domes, and Fast Runners — 16

    Predators of the Far North — 18

    Dinosaur Highways — 20

  Siberia — 21

  Canada — 22

DINOSAURS OF THE FAR SOUTH — 24

  Antarctica — 24

  Australia — 26

    Life in the Dark — 28

    Growth Rings and Footprints — 30

  New Zealand — 32

  Patagonia — 34

THE END OF THE DINOSAUR AGE — 36

The International Polar Year — 38

Where You Can See Fossils of Polar Dinosaurs — 38

Index — 39

DINOSAURS AT EARTH'S EXTREMES

One hundred and thirty million years ago, a five-ton dinosaur called *Iguanodon* (ih-GWAN-oh-don) lumbered across a sandy river plain on what is now Spitsbergen, a remote island about halfway between Norway and the North Pole. Today, Spitsbergen is covered with ice fields and glaciers, but at the time dinosaurs were alive, thick forests grew there, providing ample food for such large animals. A trail of the *Iguanodon's* giant three-toed footprints became embedded in sandstone and was preserved. When a group of geologists explored Spitsbergen in August 1960, they came upon thirteen of the 30-inch (.76-meter) tracks and were amazed. No one had ever imagined that dinosaurs once lived in polar regions. Typically, these giant reptiles were pictured in warm, tropical environments. With this discovery, people realized that dinosaurs could also live in much chillier places. In addition to the *Iguanodon* footprints found in 1960, footprints of another dinosaur, *Allosaurus* (AL-oh-SORE-us), were discovered on Spitsbergen in 1978.

Recent research in Alaska, Canada, Siberia, Antarctica, Australia, New Zealand, and Patagonia has shown that dinosaurs not only survived within the polar circles but were indeed adapted to live in these cold and seasonally dark environments. Learning about polar dinosaurs is expanding our knowledge of these amazing reptiles and helping us better understand what prehistoric life was like at Earth's extremes.

Allosaurus was a fearsome predator that walked on its hind legs and used its shorter forelimbs to grasp and tear its prey. It grew to be 30–35 feet (9–11 meters) long and weighed 1–2.5 tons (900–2250 kilograms).

Iguanodon was a large plant-eater that nipped off cycads and other plants with its sturdy beak. It grew to be about 30 feet (9.1 meters) long and about 16 feet (4.9 meters) tall.

A WARMER WORLD

Dinosaurs lived in the Mesozoic Era, a time when global climates were warmer than they are today and there was no permanent ice at the poles. The Mesozoic Era is divided into three periods: the Triassic, about 250–208 million years ago; the Jurassic, about 208–144 million years ago; and the Cretaceous, about 144–65 million years ago. In the Triassic, the Earth's climate was relatively dry, with an average global temperature of 50–60 degrees Fahrenheit (10–16 degrees Celsius). Sea levels were low, and there were deserts in the middle of the large land masses. In the Jurassic, sea levels began to rise, climates worldwide became wetter and warmer, and lush vegetation covered much of the land. In the first part of the Cretaceous, the climate became even warmer, possibly by as much as 18 degrees Fahrenheit (10 degrees Celsius), and then cooled somewhat toward the end of the period. Most fossils of polar dinosaurs are from the Cretaceous Period.

To determine what temperatures might have been in prehistoric times, scientists look at fossils, the chemical composition of rocks, records of sea levels, and other evidence. They calculate that during the Cretaceous Period, northern Alaska had a climate similar to that along the coasts of Oregon and Washington today. In southern Australia, the climate was similar to that of Fairbanks, Alaska. So even though these regions had freezing temperatures and some snow in winter, the climate was mild enough that at least some dinosaurs could live there year round.

Global climates have been changing for billions of years, warming and cooling many times. As temperatures change across the planet, patterns of life are altered, with the most dramatic effects being seen at the poles. Currently, the Earth is in a warming period following the last Ice Age, which ended about 10,000 years ago. Scientists are concerned because the climate is warming faster now than ever before. In the past one hundred years, the average world temperature has risen more than 1 degree Fahrenheit (.6 degree Celsius). As a result of warmer temperatures, there has been a decrease in the thickness and extent of Arctic sea ice, thinning of ice shelves in the Antarctic, thawing of permafrost (the permanently frozen ground found throughout the polar regions), melting of glaciers and icebergs worldwide, rising sea levels, and heavier rainfall. Polar regions are the first places where we can see the impact of climate change. They warm faster than other places on Earth because as the ice melts, the exposed dark-colored ground absorbs more of the sun's heat than the light-colored ice. This, in turn, accelerates the rate of warming. Learning more about the world's climate in the past and how life adapted to changing conditions provides information that may help us face our own future in a world of global warming.

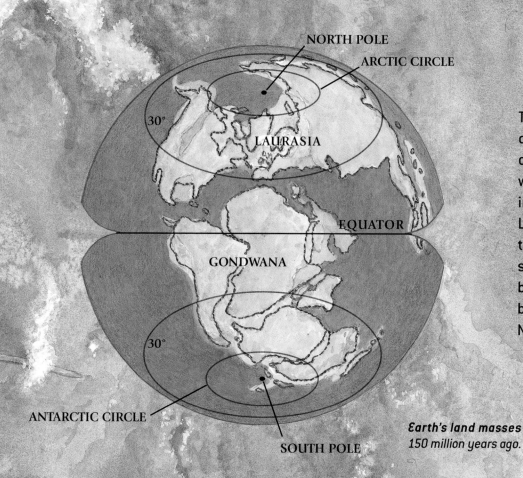

NORTH POLE

ARCTIC CIRCLE

30°

LAURASIA

EQUATOR

GONDWANA

30°

ANTARCTIC CIRCLE

SOUTH POLE

Earth's land masses 150 million years ago.

SUPERCONTINENTS

The world in the Dinosaur Age looked very different from what it is today. At the beginning of the Mesozoic Era, most of the land masses were clumped in two supercontinents, Laurasia in the north and Gondwana in the south. Over time, Laurasia and Gondwana broke apart and moved, the various pieces gradually sliding across the surface of the Earth to new positions. Laurasia became North America, Europe, and Asia. Gondwana became South America, Africa, Antarctica, Australia, New Zealand, and the Indian subcontinent.

Surviving Winter

Because of the Earth's tilt, seasons in the polar regions are extreme. In summer, the sun never sets; in winter, it never rises. The seasons are opposite in the two hemispheres, with the Arctic summer beginning in June and the Antarctic summer beginning in December. In the long days of polar summers, plant life flourishes. In the same way that caribou and reindeer and other animals today flock to the far north to feast on this bountiful food supply, dinosaurs may also have taken advantage of the seasonal abundance of food at the poles. Some of them may have migrated to polar regions each summer, returning to warmer places for winter, while others may have lived within the polar circles year round. Although some dinosaurs that stayed in polar regions remained active all winter long, others may have slowed their body processes and hibernated when the weather turned cold.

Staying Warm

While many dinosaur fossils have been found in polar regions, there have been no discoveries of bones belonging to snakes or lizards. These reptiles, whose body temperatures fluctuate with the temperature of the surrounding air, could not have survived the freezing temperatures of a polar winter. Since we know that dinosaurs did live in the cold, many scientists think that they were able to control their body temperatures to some degree. Fossil bones of some dinosaurs are filled with blood channels, a characteristic seen in the bones of warm-blooded animals. Dinosaurs may not have been warm-blooded like birds and mammals today, which are able to maintain a constant body temperature and stay warm even when the air is frigid, but they may have been able to produce or retain enough body heat to survive the cold. The recent discoveries of feathered dinosaurs in China open the possibility that some polar dinosaurs might have had feather coats to help hold in their body heat.

*On average **Troodon's** eye sockets were 2 inches (5 centimeters) across, more than twice that of other dinosaurs of similar size.*

Seeing in the Dark

Animals that live within the polar circles year round face three months without sunlight. In winter, the sky is dark, with the only light coming from the moon and the stars. How did dinosaurs see during the dark winter months as they moved about looking for food? Some, like *Troodon* (TROH-oh-don), a small meat-eating dinosaur whose fossils have been found in Alaska, had unusually large eyes. Such eyes would have made it easier for it to see in low light. Fossil skulls show that *Troodon* had an especially large brain, which would have helped it make the most of what it could see. Some dinosaurs from Australia's polar regions also had unusually big eyes.

DISCOVERING FOSSILS

In the summer of 2001, a retired geology professor visiting northern Alaska was waiting for a boat when he glanced down at the riverbank and spotted several very large bones. They turned out to be the fossilized remains of a 95-million-year-old dinosaur similar to duckbill dinosaurs that lived farther south. In 2005, a student on a college field trip to Denali National Park found a 9-inch- (23-centimeter-) long footprint of a large meat-eating dinosaur. It was the first evidence of dinosaurs discovered inside the park.

All over the world, fossils of polar dinosaurs have been found both by chance and as the result of fossil-hunting expeditions. They range from bones and teeth to trackways and skin impressions. Often, only a single tooth or bone is found, so that only the family group and not the exact species can be identified. Research is just beginning to reveal clues to the many kinds of dinosaurs that inhabited prehistoric polar regions and how these reptiles were adapted to survive. Each new discovery adds a piece to the puzzle of what the world was like millions of years ago.

Looking for fossils of polar dinosaurs has its own unique challenges. In polar regions, there are only a few months of the year when the weather is suitable for fossil hunting. Even in summer, blizzards can halt work at any time. In many cases, fossils are located in remote or largely inaccessible places. In Antarctica, scientists have to climb mountains and traverse ice floes to reach their research sites. In southern Australia, researchers have to scale seaside cliffs and battle the tides to extract buried fossils. In Alaska, most fossils are embedded in permafrost, which makes the ground ice-hard and difficult to dig. After fossils have been found and excavated, they must be encased in plaster "jackets" for protection and transported long distances to museums and universities, where they can be studied and, in some cases, prepared for display.

LIZARD HIPS AND BIRD HIPS

Scientists divide the different kinds of dinosaurs into two large groups based on their body shapes. One group, the saurischians (sore-ISS-kee-uns), whose name means "lizard hips," had hip bones shaped like those of modern lizards. It includes the giant long-necked plant-eating sauropods (SORE-oh-pods), such as *Titanosaurus* (tie-TAN-oh-SORE-uhs), and the meat-eating theropods (THAIR-oh-pods), such as *Allosaurus.* The other large group of dinosaurs, the plant-eating ornithischians (or-nith-ISS-kee-uns), or "bird hips," named for their bird like hips, includes dinosaurs such as *Iguanodon.* Fossils found in polar regions represent all of the dinosaur groups.

DINOSAURS OF THE FAR NORTH

Alaska

Dinosaur fossils were first collected in Alaska in 1961 by Robert Liscomb, an oil-company geologist who was surveying land along the Colville River on Alaska's North Slope, the treeless plain north of the Brooks Range. At the time, Liscomb thought the fossils were from mammoths and other Ice Age animals. He died in a rock slide a year later, and it was not until 1984 that the bones were identified as belonging to dinosaurs. Since then, thousands of dinosaur fossils from more than a dozen species have been discovered in northern Alaska. It is the richest source of polar dinosaur fossils in the world.

As the Colville River winds its way across the coastal plain of northern Alaska, it cuts through layers of frozen land. In winter, the river is solid ice, but in summer, the water flows and sun melts the permafrost exposed along its banks, which erode and often reveal buried dinosaur bones. Every year scientists find new fossils along the river's shore. In the summer of 2007, researchers dug a 66-foot- (20-meter-) long tunnel into the bluff along the riverbank just above the Liscomb bone deposits. Inside the tunnel, they dug into the frozen ground and excavated more than one hundred specimens. Even though the tunnel was dark and cold, it allowed scientists to work when bad weather made excavating fossils outdoors impossible.

Almost all of the fossils from northern Alaska are from the Cretaceous Period, and most are from animals that lived 75 to 70 million years ago. Fossils of leaves and pine needles tell us that this part of Alaska was covered in forest at the time. Dinosaur fossils have been found in a number of other places in Alaska as well, including the Talkeetna Mountains and the Alaska Peninsula.

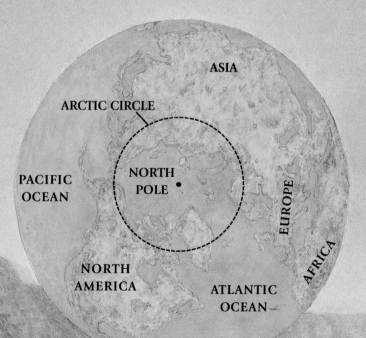

Earth's northern hemisphere. *Dinosaur fossils have been found in Arctic regions of North America, Europe, and Asia.*

A Herd of Hadrosaurs

The most common Alaskan dinosaur fossils are of a hadrosaur (HAD-roh-sore), or duckbill dinosaur, called *Edmontosaurus* (ed-MON-toh-SORE-us), a huge plant-eater the size of a school bus. Large numbers of fossils have been found together and include bones from dinosaurs of various ages, suggesting that these animals lived in herds. The *Edmontosaurus* herds probably stayed in the far north year round, because the young animals born during the summer season would not have been strong enough to migrate long distances. Even though food would have been harder to find in winter, evergreens, bark, and water plants would have been available. Duckbills broke off pieces of plants with their beaks. Their large jaws were filled with sturdy teeth, which were good for eating tough fibers.

Fossil remains of other Alaskan hadrosaurs include those of *Kritosaurus* (KRITE-oh-SORE-us), a smaller relative of *Edmontosaurus*, and a type of lambeosaurid (LAMB-ee-oh-SORE-id), a hadrosaur with a bony crest on its head.

Edmontosaurus stood 10 feet (3 meters) tall and weighed between 3000 and 4000 pounds (1350 and 1800 kilograms). Like other hadrosaurs, it ran upright on its sturdy back legs, using its large, stiff tail for balance. When grazing, it may have walked on all fours.

Crests, Domes, and Fast Runners

In 1994, fossil bones of a large plant-eating dinosaur called *Pachyrhinosaurus* (PAK-ee-RINE-oh-SORE-us) were discovered along the Colville River. This dinosaur is a rare member of the ceratops (SER-a-tops) family, which includes the well-known *Triceratops* (try-SER-a-tops). *Pachyrhinosaurus* had a frill around its neck and a bony knob on its face, which it may have used in butting or shoving matches with others of its own kind. When scientists recently returned to the site where the bones had been found, the remains of eight more pachyrhinosaurs were revealed. All were

Pachyrhinosaurus was 7 feet (2.1 meters) tall and 18 feet (5.5 meters) long, and it weighed up to 4 tons (3.6 metric tons), or as much as a pickup truck.

close in age, and they had probably died together in a flood or other natural catastrophe. Like the duckbills, these dinosaurs apparently roamed the Alaskan landscape in herds. Fossil bones of another member of the ceratops family, *Anchiceratops* (AN-ki-SER-a-tops), have also been found in Alaska.

Another large Alaskan plant-eater, *Pachycephalosaurus* (PAK-ee-sef-a-loe-SORE-us), was distinguished by its thick dome-shaped skull, which was once thought to have been used for butting other dinosaurs. However, recent research suggests that the helmetlike head covering was probably used for communication or for display during the mating season. This dinosaur may also have had a decorative comb or crest on its head.

Thescelosaurus (thes-kel-oh-SORE-us) was a small, swift dinosaur that ran on its long hind legs, gripping the ground with its clawed feet. Its long tail helped it keep its balance while turning quickly. It is a member of the hypsilophodontid (HIP-see-lo-fo-DON-tid) family, a group also found in southern polar regions. These plant-eaters had unusually large eyes, good for seeing in the dark.

Thescelosaurus was a human-sized dinosaur about 5 feet (1.5 meters) tall, weighing about 200 pounds (90 kilograms).

Pachycephalosaurus stood about 7 feet (2.1 meters) tall, was 15 feet (4.6 meters) long, and weighed about 300 pounds (135 kilograms).

Dromaeosaurus stood about 4 feet (1.2 meters) tall, was 6 feet (1.8 meters) long, and weighed about 100 pounds (45 kilograms).

Troodons in Alaska stood about 6 feet (1.8 meters) tall, nearly twice the size of Troodons found in warmer locations. Their larger size would have been better for retaining body heat.

Predators of the Far North

The plant-eaters of prehistoric Alaska were preyed upon by the theropod, or meat-eating, dinosaurs. The most common predator was *Troodon*. At one site, 42 of its sharp, jagged teeth were found. *Troodon* used its short, clawed forelimbs for grasping and its slender back legs for walking. On each foot was a large sickle-shaped claw, a dangerous weapon that could be used like a knife to slice open its victims. *Troodon* probably ate whatever it could find, including small dinosaurs, mammals, and plants.

The tyrannosaurids (tie-RAN-oh-SORE-ids) were the largest Alaskan predators. They include two close relatives of the fearsome *Tyrannosaurus*

Albertosaurus, whose bones were first found in Alberta, Canada, grew to a length of 28 feet (8.5 meters), was 13 feet (4 meters) tall, and weighed 2.5 tons (2.3 metric tons).

rex (tie-RAN-oh-SORE-us rex)—*Tyrannosaurus* and *Albertosaurus* (al-BERT-oh-SORE-us). All of the tyrannosaurids had heavy bodies, huge heads, and jaws filled with sharp, pointed teeth. These powerful, fast-moving dinosaurs were the top predators of the Cretaceous Period.

The dromaeosaurids (DROH-may-oh-SORE-ids) were small, speedy dinosaurs that ran on long legs. Fossils from this group found in Alaska include bones of *Dromaeosaurus* (DROH-may-oh-SORE-us) and *Saurornith-olestes* (sore-OR-nith-oh-LES-teez), a similar species. These fierce predators probably hunted in groups, much like a pack of wolves.

Dinosaur Highways

In the summer of 1998, as a group of scientists traveled by boat down a 120-mile (193-kilometer) stretch of the Colville River searching the shoreline for traces of dinosaurs, they discovered thirteen sites with dinosaur footprints. The tracks, which were 90 to 110 million years old, represented five different types of dinosaurs, both meat-eaters and plant-eaters. The largest footprint, 18 inches (46 centimeters) long, was made by a member of the tyrannosaur family. Other smaller, three-toed, bird-like tracks were from duckbill dinosaurs and their relatives. The scientists also found one four-toed print, typical of an armored dinosaur. One unusual track showed the pebbly texture of the dinosaur's scaly skin.

The earliest evidence of dinosaurs in Alaska is a set of 140-million-year-old footprints found in the Black Lake area on the Alaska Peninsula. The fourteen three-toed prints were probably made by two different theropod dinosaurs. Dinosaur tracks have been found elsewhere as well, including the discovery of a 14-inch (36-centimeter) duckbill footprint in southwest Alaska.

Dinosaur footprints and trackways provide information about different types of dinosaurs and their sizes and show us how these animals moved across the Alaskan landscape. Tracks grouped together show that some dinosaurs traveled in herds or packs. The distance between footprints indicates whether the animals were walking or running. It is thought that some dinosaurs may have moved between North America (Alaska) and Asia (Siberia), crossing a land bridge at the Bering Strait. Further research will look for evidence of how and when they might have done this.

Titanosaurs. Their name means "giant reptile."

Siberia

Fossils of polar dinosaurs discovered in Siberia include the remains of meat-eating allosaurs and troodontids, as well as plant-eating ceratopsians, hadrosaurs, and sauropods. Recently, scientists excavated the bones of a huge sauropod foot. They belonged to a titanosaur (tie-TAN-oh-sore), one of the largest dinosaurs to ever walk the Earth. These animals could weigh up to 100 tons (91 metric tons) and grow to be 40 yards (36 meters) long, nearly half the length of a football field. One species made footprints 3 feet (.9 meter) wide. Fragments of titanosaur skeletons have been found at several other Siberian sites as well. It is the farthest north that these huge dinosaurs are known to have lived.

Canada

The far northern parts of Canada were also home to polar dinosaurs. The first dinosaur bones from the Canadian Arctic were discovered in 1987 on Bylot Island, an area of rugged mountains, ice fields, and glaciers off the northern coast of Baffin Island. Researchers who had gone there to collect fossils of plant spores and pollen found bones of duckbills and a theropod dinosaur as well. Bylot Island is now a land of ice and snow, but fossil pollen tells us that it was covered in forest 70 million years ago, when dinosaurs lived there.

In 2003, another expedition went to Bylot Island. Trekking across rocks and tundra in howling winds and near-freezing temperatures, the researchers scanned the ground for dinosaur remains. They discovered a fossilized tyrannosaur foot bone belonging to a huge animal up to 33 feet (10 meters) long and possibly weighing as much as 5500 pounds (2475 kilograms). It was the first evidence of these predatory dinosaurs this far north. Elsewhere in northern Canada, the remains of ceratopsian dinosaurs have been found in the Northwest Territories; duckbill fossils have also been discovered in the Yukon Territory and on Ellesmere Island. Researchers in the Canadian Arctic are currently studying fossil remains to learn more about global climate change.

Duckbill dinosaurs may have foraged in herds.

Tyrannosaurs were among the largest known predatory dinosaurs.

23

DINOSAURS OF THE FAR SOUTH

Antarctica

In the summer of 1991, scientists at Mount Kirkpatrick, a 13,000-foot- (4000-meter-) high peak near the South Pole, discovered the 190-million-year-old fossil bones of a dinosaur they named *Cryolophosaurus ellioti* (CRY-oh-lo-fo-SORE-us el-ee-AH-tee). This meat-eater, similar to the fearsome *Allosaurus* from the northern hemisphere, was the first carnivore found in Antarctica. The crest on the dinosaur's head, which was probably used for display during the mating season, earned it the nickname "Elvisaurus." At the time that Elvisaurus was alive, the rocks in which its bones were found were part of a riverbed on the southern coast of Gondwana. Over time, as continents shifted and land pushed up, the fossils became part of a mountain. In 2004, scientists returned by helicopter to the site to continue excavating the fossil. While they were digging, the mountaineer who accompanied them discovered the bones of another dinosaur nearby. It turned out to be a large sauropod—possibly the last meal of *Cryolophosaurus*. The sauropod is a new species, previously unknown in Antarctica.

Another new Antarctic species, currently known as the "Naze theropod," after the region where it was found, was also discovered in 2004. To dig out the fossils, scientists had to walk 8 miles (13 kilometers) a day across treacherous ice floes to reach the site. The Naze theropod lived about 70 million years ago, a time when the climate in Antarctica was similar to that of the Pacific Northwest today and the land was covered in a thick forest of cycads, palms, and ginkgos. Eight types of dinosaurs have been discovered in Antarctica. Among them are fossils of an ankylosaur (ANK-ee-lo-sore), a kind of armored dinosaur, which were found in 1986 on James Ross Island, and fossils of a hypsilophodont from Vega Island.

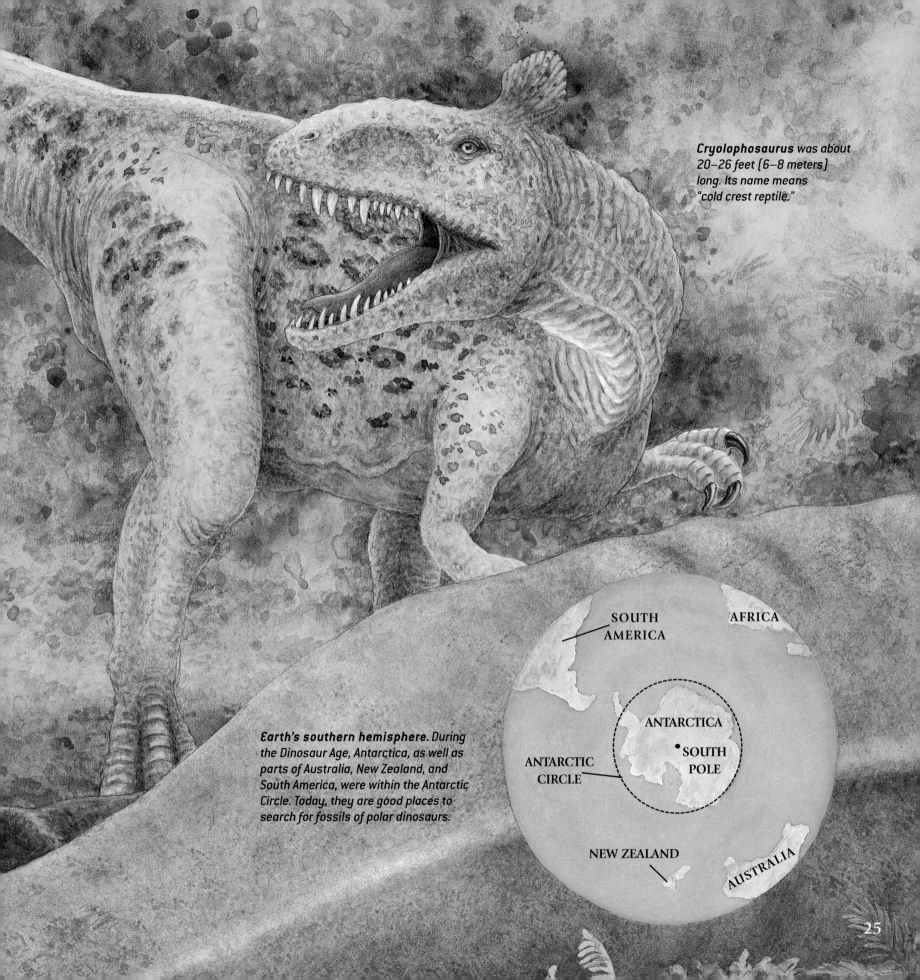

Cryolophosaurus was about 20–26 feet (6–8 meters) long. Its name means "cold crest reptile."

Earth's southern hemisphere. During the Dinosaur Age, Antarctica, as well as parts of Australia, New Zealand, and South America, were within the Antarctic Circle. Today, they are good places to search for fossils of polar dinosaurs.

SOUTH AMERICA

AFRICA

ANTARCTICA

ANTARCTIC CIRCLE

SOUTH POLE

NEW ZEALAND

AUSTRALIA

25

Australia

In 1924, workers at a large sheep station, or ranch, in southwestern Queensland discovered a huge fossil skeleton eroding out of the ground. They dug out some of the pieces and sent them to the Queensland Museum in Brisbane, where they were identified as belonging to a new type of sauropod dinosaur. It was given the name *Rhoetosaurus brownei* (reet-oh-SORE-us BROWN-ee). It was one of the first known Australian dinosaurs. *Rhoetosaurus* was a gigantic dinosaur weighing up to 22 tons (20 metric tons), or as much as four elephants. It supported its massive weight on huge tree trunk–shaped legs, and it would have defended itself against predators by swinging its long tail from side to side like a whip. This plant-eater used its long neck to reach leaves on the tops of trees, much as modern giraffes do. When *Rhoetosaurus* was alive 180 million years ago, Australia was connected to the rest of Gondwana by Antarctica, and this part of Queensland was at or near the polar circle. Today, southern Queensland is near the tropics.

Rhoetosaurus grew to be more than 50 feet (15 meters) long and was 10–13 feet (3–4 meters) tall at the hips. It is one of the oldest known sauropods in the world.

27

Life in the Dark

The richest source of polar dinosaur fossils in Australia and in the southern hemisphere is along the southern coast of Australia in the state of Victoria. Two sites there have yielded more than 5000 fossils of more than a dozen kinds of dinosaurs. At Dinosaur Cove in the Otway Ranges, researchers, assisted by hundreds of volunteers, drilled into a seaside cliff while waves crashed behind them in order to extract the fossils. At Flat Rocks, near Inverloch, another seaside site, bones were found embedded in an ancient streambed that had become part of the rocky shoreline. Most of the Victorian fossils are from animals that lived 105 to 115 million years ago, and the vast majority belonged to small, large-eyed dinosaurs called hypsilophodontids. They lived in a forest of pine and ginkgo trees and probably fed on ferns, horsetails (segmented reedlike plants), and other low-lying plants. These dinosaurs get their name from their high-crested teeth, which were good for cutting and chewing tough leaves and stems. As the teeth wore down from use, new ones grew in to replace them.

With good vision in low light, the hypsilophodontids may have fed at twilight or at night, when daytime predators were less active. They could run fast on their long legs and probably relied on speed to escape from danger. One of the best preserved fossils is of a small dinosaur called *Leaellynosaura* (lay-EL-lin-oh-SORE-a). The unusual feature of this dinosaur's fossil skull is that it contains a cast, or mold, of the brain, which shows exceptionally large optic lobes, the part of the brain connected to the eyes. This reinforces the idea that hypsilophodontids were adapted for life in the dark. Other species of hypsilophodontids found on the Victorian coast include *Atlascopcosaurus* (AT-lus-COP-co-SORE-us) and *Fulgurotherum* (FUL-goo-roe-THEE-rum).

Leaellynosaura was named after the daughter of its discoverers, Pat and Tom Rich. The bones are from a young animal about 2.5 feet (.75 meter) long. An adult would have grown to be nearly 3 feet (.9 meter) long.

Growth Rings and Footprints

Fossils of a small theropod called *Timimus* (TIM-ee-mus) have also been found in southeastern Australia. The long leg bones show that it was a speedy runner. Cross sections of the bones have rings similar to the growth rings in trees. Thick rings formed during periods of rapid growth; thin rings, when growth stopped or slowed down. This pattern is typical in the bones of animals that hibernate, which suggests that *Timimus* survived winter by becoming inactive. Perhaps this dinosaur found a sheltered spot under a tree or beneath a rock ledge, curled up, and went to sleep until spring.

Timimus grew to about 11.5 feet (3.5 meters) long and 5 feet (1.5 meters) tall.

The bones of hypsilophodontids, on the other hand, have no growth rings, indicating that these animals were active throughout the year. It is thought that they stayed in the polar regions of Australia year round. Even if they had wanted to migrate to warmer climates, they could not have done so easily because a shallow inland sea blocked the most direct route north.

The recent discovery of three fossil footprints provides proof that large predatory dinosaurs also roamed southern Australia 115 million years ago. The three-toed prints measure about 14 inches (36 centimeters) long and were made by an animal about 12 feet (3.7 meters) tall, or about the size of a small adult *Tyrannosaurus*. A thick layer of fat may have helped these animals keep warm in winter. Other dinosaurs represented by fossils found in southern Australia include *Allosaurus,* a dromaeosaurid, and other species that are still in the process of being identified.

*With good eyesight, **Hypsilophodontids** would have been able to find food even during the dark months of winter.*

New Zealand

Until the unlikely discovery of an odd-looking bone in 1975, no one ever imagined that dinosaur fossils could be found in New Zealand. Not only was the climate thought to be too cold for dinosaurs, but the islands were believed to be too small to support such large animals. In addition, New Zealand was under water much of the time during the Dinosaur Age.

Joan Wiffen, an amateur fossil hunter now known as the "dragon lady," proved the scientists wrong. She loved rocks and learned about them by reading books, taking classes, talking to experts, and studying geology maps. In 1972, she found an old map that reported bones of reptiles along a streambed in the Te Hoe Valley. A coastal estuary during dinosaur times, this valley is now in the mountains about 70 miles (113 kilometers) inland from Hawkes Bay. Joan and her family went there, scrambled down the rocky embankments, and discovered all sorts of fossils—mainly of fish, shells, turtles, huge sea reptiles called mosasaurs, and other ocean life. One day in 1975, after Joan's husband cracked open a rock, she spotted an unusual vertebra, or backbone. She had never seen anything like it before. It turned out to be a tailbone of a meat-eating dinosaur similar to *Tyrannosaurus rex*. Since then, at least four groups of dinosaurs have been discovered in the Te Hoe Valley. All are fragments of skeletons. Yet they prove that dinosaurs did, indeed, walk millions of years ago on the land that became New Zealand.

Joan Wiffen was the first to discover dinosaur fossils in New Zealand.

33

Patagonia

The southern tip of South America was close to or within the Antarctic Circle during most of the Dinosaur Age, and it was home to a variety of dinosaurs. In 2004, Argentine scientists announced the discovery of the nearly complete skeleton of a new long-necked plant-eating dinosaur that roamed the southwestern Patagonian landscape about 70 million years ago. They named the dinosaur *Talenkauen santacrucensis* (TAL-en-COW-en SAN-ta-cru-SEN-sis). "Talenkauen" means "small head" in the local Aonikenk Indian language. Bones of meat-eating and giant plant-eating sauropod dinosaurs were found nearby, as well as an abundance of petrified logs of large evergreen trees, evidence that these animals lived in a thick forest. The discovery of *Talenkauen* is significant because it is one of just a few ornithischian dinosaurs found in this region. Unlike the more common sauropods, which fed high in the trees, these dinosaurs ate plants closer to the ground and chewed their food before swallowing it. An unusual feature of *Talenkauen* is bony platelike structures in the chest. Scientists are studying them to determine what their function might have been. Other fossils found in the same area include bones of fish, turtles, and crocodiles, a sign that there were freshwater rivers and lakes as well.

Talenkauen was a type of iguanodont that grew to be 13 feet (4 meters) long. It walked on its sturdy back legs and used its five-fingered hands to grasp branches and leaves.

THE END OF THE DINOSAUR AGE

Discoveries of dinosaur bones in the polar regions of the Mesozoic Era show scientists that these giant reptiles were more complex and widespread than was previously thought. The findings have added new information about dinosaurs and raised questions about their extinction 65 million years ago.

Dinosaurs disappeared about the same time that a huge asteroid crashed into the Earth. That impact would have created an enormous dust cloud, blocking all sunlight and plunging the world into months of cold and darkness. Until the discovery of polar dinosaurs, it was thought that dinosaurs could not have survived in such a hostile environment and that the asteroid was the main reason they became extinct. Now we know that at least some dinosaurs *could* live in such a dark and chilly world. Scientists currently think that it was a combination of factors, including a major shift in the world's climate at the end of the Cretaceous Period, that caused the extinction of dinosaurs and so many other animals.

Dinosaurs reigned for 150 million years, at a time when the Earth's climate was much warmer than it is today. They inhabited almost every corner of the planet, including the polar regions. They are one of Earth's most successful animal groups. As we continue to learn more, we will gain a new perspective on these diverse and fascinating prehistoric reptiles and the world in which they lived. And as we add to our knowledge of polar dinosaurs, it will help us understand how so many different species have been able to adapt and thrive at Earth's extremes.

THE INTERNATIONAL POLAR YEAR

Polar regions play a key role in global climates and are among the first places to show signs of changes that can affect ecosystems worldwide. Research at the poles can help us understand how such changes occurred in the past, and what we might expect in the future. The year 2007–08 was designated as an International Polar Year (IPY) by the International Council of Science and the World Meteorological Organisation. This was the fourth IPY, with previous ones held in 1882–83, 1932–33, and 1957–58. In that last year, polar studies were incorporated into the International Geophysical Year. An IPY is an intense, coordinated campaign of research, involving scientists from a wide range of disciplines. The 2007–08 IPY actually lasted from March 1, 2007, to March 1, 2009, to include two seasons of research at each pole. It involved scientists from sixty-three countries, including the United States and Canada, who conducted more than two hundred separate studies ranging from the effect of solar radiation on the polar atmosphere and exotic marine life swimming beneath Antarctic ice to glacial melting and polar dinosaurs. IPY brought a worldwide focus on the Earth's polar regions with the goal of developing an ongoing awareness of their importance. More information about IPY can be found at *www.ipy.org* or *www.us-ipy.org*.

WHERE YOU CAN SEE FOSSILS OF POLAR DINOSAURS

Fossils of polar dinosaurs are on exhibit in just a few museums worldwide. If you cannot visit one of these museums in person, you can learn about some of their displays at their websites.

Alaska Museum of Natural History, Eagle River, Alaska
   (www.alaskamuseum.org)
Fryxell Geology Museum, Augustana College, Science Building, Rock Island, Illinois
   (www.augustana.edu/academics/geology/department/fryxell.htm)
Museum of Nature and Science, Dallas, Texas
   (www.natureandscience.org)
Museum Victoria, Melbourne, Australia
   (museumvictoria.com.au/)
Paleontological Museum, University of Oslo, Norway
   (www.toyen.uio.no/palmus/english.htm)
Queensland Museum, Brisbane, Australia
   (www.qm.qld.gov.au/features/dinosaurs/)
University of Alaska Museum of the North, Fairbanks, Alaska
   (www.uaf.edu/museum/)
For more information about Alaskan dinosaurs, go to:
   www.blm.gov/ak/st/en/prog/culture/dinosaurs.html
For information about and preview of the PBS program "Arctic Dinosaurs" and
   links to books and related sites, go to: www.pbs.org/wgbh/nova/arcticdino/

Index

Africa, 7, 13, 25

Alaska, 2, 4, 6, 9–10, 12–14, 17–20, 38

Antarctic, 7–8, 38

Antarctic Circle, 7, 25, 34

Antarctica, 4, 7, 10, 24–26

Arctic, 7–8, 13, 22

Arctic Circle, 7, 13

Asia, 7, 13, 20

Australia, 2, 4, 6–7, 9–10, 25–26, 28,
    30–31, 38

Baffin Island, 22

Bering Strait, 20

Bylot Island, 22

Canada, 4, 19, 22, 38

climate, 6–7, 22, 24, 31–32, 36, 38

Colville River, 12–13, 16, 20

Cretaceous Period, 6, 13, 19, 36

Denali National Park, 10

Dinosaur
  bones, 8, 10–14, 16–17, 19, 21–22,
    24, 28–32, 34, 36
  brains, 9, 28
  crests, 14, 16–17, 24–25
  eyes, 9, 17, 28, 31
  feathers, 8
  feet, 17–18, 21–22
  food, 4, 8–9, 14, 31, 34
  footprints, 4, 10, 20–21, 30–31
  herds, 14, 17, 20, 22
  legs, 4, 15, 17–19, 26, 28, 30, 35
  meat-eating, 9–11, 18–21, 24,
    32, 34
  necks, 11, 16, 26, 34

plant-eating, 5, 11, 14, 16–21,
    26, 34

skeletons, 21, 26, 32, 34

skin impressions, 10, 20

skulls, 9, 17, 28

tails, 15, 17, 26

teeth, 10, 14, 18–19, 28

tracks, 4, 10, 20

Dinosaur Age, 7, 25, 32, 34, 36

Dinosaur Cove, 28

Europe, 7, 13

Flat Rocks, 28

forests, 4, 13, 22, 24, 28, 34

fossils, 4, 6, 8–14, 16–17, 19, 21–22,
    24–26, 28, 30–34, 38

geologists, 4, 10, 12

Gondwana, 7, 24, 26

hibernation, 8, 30

ice, 4, 7, 10, 13, 22, 24, 38

Ice Age, 6, 12

International Polar Year, 38

Jurassic Period, 6–7

Laurasia, 7

Liscomb, Robert, 12–13

migration, 14, 31

Mesozoic Era, 6–7, 36

New Zealand, 4, 7, 24–25, 32–33

North America, 7, 13, 20
North Pole, 4, 7, 13
Norway, 4, 38

ornithischians, 11, 34
    ankylosaurs, 24
    ceratopsians, 16–17, 21–22
        Anchiceratops, 17
        Pachyrhinosaurus, 16
        Triceratops, 16
    duckbills, 10, 14, 17, 20, 22
        (see hadrosaurs)
    hadrosaurs, 14–15, 21
        (see duckbills)
        Edmontosaurus, 14–15
        lambeosaurids, 14
        Kritosaurus, 14
    hypsilophodontids, 17, 24, 28, 31
        Atlascopcosaurus, 28
        Fulgurotherum, 28
        Leaellynosaura, 28–29
        Thescelosaurus, 17
    iguanodonts, 35
        Iguanodon, 4–5, 11
        Talenkauen santacrucensis, 34, 35
        Pachycephalosaurus, 17

Patagonia, 4, 34
permafrost, 7, 10, 13
plants, 5, 8, 14, 18, 22, 28, 34
polar circles, 4, 8–9, 13, 25–26
polar regions, 4, 7–11, 17, 31, 36, 38
predators, 4, 18–19, 22–23, 28, 31

Queensland, 26, 38

reptiles, 4, 8, 10, 21, 25, 32, 36
Rich, Patricia Vickers, 2, 29

Rich, Tom, 2, 29

saurischians, 11
    sauropods, 11, 21, 24, 26–27, 34
        Rhoetosaurus brownei, 26–27
    titanosaurs, 21
        Titanosaurus, 11
    theropods, 11, 18, 20, 22, 30
    allosaurs, 21
        Allosaurus, 4, 11, 24, 31
        Cryolophosaurus ellioti, 24–25
    dromaeosaurids, 19, 31
        Dromeosaurus, 18–19
        Saurornitholestes, 19
    Naze theropod, 24
    Timimus, 30
    troodontids, 21
        Troodon, 9, 18
    tyrannosaurids, 18, 20, 22
        Albertosaurus, 19
        Tyrannosaurus, 19, 23, 31
        Tyrannosaurus rex, 18, 32
scientists, 2, 6, 8, 10–11, 13, 16, 20–21,
    24, 32, 34, 36, 38
Siberia, 4, 20–21
South America, 7, 25, 34
South Pole, 7, 24–25
Spitsbergen, 4
summer, 8, 10, 13–14, 20, 24

Triassic Period, 6

United States, 38

Victoria, 2, 28, 38

Wiffen, Joan, 32–33
winter, 6, 8–9, 13–14, 30–31